World's Greatest
ENTREPRENEURS

(An imprint of Prakash Books)

(An imprint of Prakash Books)

contact@wonderhousebooks.com

© Wonder House Books 2025

All rights reserved. No part of this book may be reproduced or
transmitted in any form by any means, electronic or mechanical
including photocopying and recording, or by any information
storage and retrieval system except as may be expressly permitted
in writing by the publisher.

ISBN : 9789388810371

CONTENTS

AMANCIO ORTEGA GAONA

BIRTH: March 28, 1936
León, Spain

Amancio Ortega is a Spanish fashion entre-preneur and founder of popular fashion chains such as Zara, Pull&Bear and Oysho.

Amancio Ortega Gaona was born on March 28, 1936, in León, Spain. He is the youngest of four children. When he was fourteen, his family moved to A Coruña in Spain due to their financial situation. His father was a railway worker. His mother was a housemaid. Amancio started working at a very young age.

To support his family, he got a job in the textile industry as an employee of two well-known clothing stores. He worked as a shirt-maker and there he learned the art of making clothes. He left high school at the age of fourteen. He never received any higher education. Ortega continued working in the textile field until the early 1960s. While there, he learned the basics of business as well. He studied how products and costs changed when they traveled from the manufacturer to the consumer. Ortega realized that to earn good money, one should give customers what they really want. He worked in the industry for ten years before launching his own company.

In 1963, at the age of 27, he started Confecciones Goa. The business was successful and provided excellent quality bath robes at very low costs. In 1975, Ortega opened his first retail store called 'Zara'. Zara sells clothes for men, women and children, like most other fashion brands. But what they did differently was to produce clothing that the customers really wanted, cost-effectively, in a short span of time. Another unique feature of Zara was that they never reproduced their most successful pieces.

These hits were simply modified and offered in different versions.

Zara became a massive success for providing clothing at low prices with express delivery. The brand was simple and direct. Ortega aimed to bring runway clothes to the common consumer in a few weeks' time. Zara became so popular that the company didn't even need advertising.

In 1985, Ortega opened Inditex as the holding company for Zara. Inditex became one of the largest textile companies in the world. The Inditex Group now has over 92,000 employees.

Ortega fully expanded his business in the early 90s. After opening his stores in Spain, he launched Zara shops in Portugal, where the workforce was cheaper. Ortega expanded his business further and created brands like Pull&Bear, Bershka, Oysho and Massimo Dutti. By 2000 he had reached more than thirty markets. The Inditex Group went public in 2001. Ortega had larger stakes in the company making him one of the wealthiest men in the world.

Ortega also dabbles in investments and charitable work. Apart from investing his time and capital in the fashion industry, he has made investments in gas, banks, tourism, and real estate. With his wife, he founded The Paideia Foundation in 1986. The organization provides education to people with mental and physical disabilities. In 2001, he created another NGO called Fundación Amancio Ortega. It aims to promote science, research, education, social action, and culture.

Despite being a notable name in the fashion industry, he always keeps a low profile. He made very few public appearances. In fact, till 1999, most media outlets had not even published Ortega's photograph. Ortega always avoids interviews and publicity. He is said to be a workaholic who has not taken a holiday for 25 years. He is known to spend millions to keep his life private. Due to this fact, no one has too many details about his first marriage to Rosalía Mera who was his first business partner. The couple had two children. He divorced his first wife in 1986 and got married for the second time in 2001 to Flora Pérez Marcote. Flora's daughter is considered to be Ortega's successor.

Ortega's life story shows that he achieved his success through sheer self-confidence and hard work. He created an unshakable trust with his customers which led him to incomparable success.

ANDREW CARNEGIE

BIRTH: November 25, 1835
Dunfermline, Scotland

DEATH: August 11, 1919 (aged 83)
Lenox, Massachusetts, USA

Andrew Carnegie was a Scottish-American steel tycoon and one of the wealthiest businessmen of the nineteenth century.

Andrew Carnegie was born on November 25, 1835, in Dunfermline, Scotland to William Carnegie and Margaret Morrison Carnegie. His father was a weaver, and Carnegie grew up in a family who gave importance to books and learning. When Andrew was thirteen, he moved to the United States with his family in 1848. Due to his family's financial conditions he ended up working in cotton factories. But he left his job and started focusing on reading, theater and music. In 1849, he became a messenger boy for a telegraph office in Pittsburgh.

In 1853, Carnegie took up a job at the Pennsylvania Railroad. He worked there with Thomas A. Scott as a personal telegrapher and assistant. He started to understand the importance of iron and steel. The railroad business was the top-rated business in America in those days. During the civil war, iron bridges were in high demand. Working with Scott was a learning milestone for Carnegie; he learned the basics of investment. In 1856, Theodore Woodruff approached Carnegie with an idea to create sleeping cars on the railways. He also gave him a small part of the Woodruff Sleeping Car Company. Carnegie accepted the offer and invested in his idea. He was the first person to introduce the sleeping car in the U.S. railways.

In 1861, Carnegie invested in oil. The money that he got from his sleeping cars was spent on buying an oil company. This led Carnegie to expand his wealth. In 1865, he left his railroad job to focus on other interests. That year he founded the Keystone Bridge Company. Carnegie began reaching out, to make contacts and profits in the iron-making industry. He took every other project out there to build bridges.

In mid 1870s, Carnegie opened his first steel plant in Pennsylvania. He purchased a rival steel company called the Homestead Steel Works. In 1892, he established the Carnegie Steel Company. To open the company, he used the money he had amassed over the years. His company worked to create many technological inventions in the production of steel. Carnegie achieved success and became the biggest manufacturer of pig iron, steel rails, and coke in the world. In 1901, Carnegie sold his steel company to J.P. Morgan. Morgan created the U.S. Steel Corporation and made Carnegie the richest man in the world.

Carnegie began his charitable work in 1870. He supported multiple projects and causes. He is best known for his contribution to free public library buildings. He gifted libraries to the English-speaking world like the US, UK, Australia, and New Zealand. Even though he was considered to be the richest man, his philosophy was to use little on himself and instead use his great wealth to promote the welfare and happiness of others. For these noble intentions, Carnegie was widely praised.

Carnegie provided funds for the Carnegie Trust. In 1895, he established a university called the Carnegie Institute of Pittsburgh. He also donated money to build the Carnegie Institute of Technology (CIT) at Pittsburgh in 1901. Besides the obvious infrastructure, the institute includes an art gallery, music hall and a museum. To encourage research and development, he began the Carnegie Institution of Washington.

In 1886, he published his well-known piece *Triumphant Democracy*. It was well-accepted in the U.S. In 1889, he wrote *The Gospel of Wealth* in which he describes the social differences between the wealthy class and the less fortunate in the society.

Carnegie got married in 1887 to Louise Whitfield at the age of 51. He had only one child. He died of bronchial pneumonia on August 11, 1919, in Massachusetts.

ARIANNA HUFFINGTON

BIRTH: July 15, 1950
Athens, Greece

Arianna Huffington is an author, philanthropist and television personality. She is the owner of online news magazine, *The Huffington Post*.

Arianna Huffington, originally Arianna Stassinopoulos, was born on July 15, 1950, in Athens, Greece to Konstantinos and Elli Stasinopoulos. Her father was a journalist and a management consultant. She was close to her father, but she was influenced more by her mother. At the age of sixteen, Arianna moved to the UK. She studied Economics at Girton College, Cambridge. She joined the college debating society called the Cambridge Union. She was the first foreign, and third female president of the society. She graduated in 1972 with a Master's degree.

After her graduation, Huffington appeared in an edition of *Face the Music* along with Bernard Levin. Levin helped her with the editing, and soon she started writing books. She also worked as a columnist, critic, and a television host. Her career took off with the release of *The Female Woman* in 1973. The book was a bestseller and brought her a lot of fame. She came up with her second book, *After Reason,* in 1978 which was not as successful as the first one. After this, she turned to *Vogue, Cosmopolitan,* and newspapers like the *Daily Mail* and *The Spectator.*

Due to some personal issues, she moved to New York in 1980 and began to take an interest in politics and journalism. In the late 1980s, Huffington wrote several articles for the *National Review.* Her next big hit was a biographical book on Maria Callas called *Maria*

Callas – The Woman Behind the Legend in 1980. In 1983, she released *The Gods of Greece*. She also wrote a biography of Pablo Picasso called *Picasso: Creator and Destroyer* in 1988.

Apart from writing, she was also a member of the Republican Party. She became famous for being a strong supporter of conservative causes. She made regular television appearances to state and support her viewpoints. Later on, she started to shift towards more environmental causes and corporate improvement. In 1998, she began to do a weekly radio show called *Left, Right, and Centre*. In 2003 she started the 'Detroit Project'.

The year 2005 was the turning point in Huffington's career. She launched *The Huffington Post* that year. Before starting her blog, she hosted a website called *Ariannaonline.com*. However, her first venture on the Internet was a website called *Resignation.com*.

Huffington became the editor-in-chief of The Huffington Post Media Group after six years.

The Huffington Post now covers a wide variety of topics like politics, sports and business. In 2008, *The Observer* named it as the most powerful blog in the world. Aside from her business, she was part of the cast of the animated series *The Cleveland Show*. She gave her voice to the wife of Tim the bear, also named Arianna. She made a few appearances on shows such as *Roseanne, The L Word, How I Met Your Mother, Help Me Help You,* and in the film *EdTV*.

Huffington's major works include her participation in the '24th Annual Distinguished Speaker Series' in 2010. She has appeared several times in the news for her debates on world events, political issues, and the local economy. In 2011, Arianna sold *The Huffington Post* to AOL. She became the President and editor-in-chief of The Huffington Post Media Group. In 2016, she announced that she was leaving the company to start a health and wellness company called Thrive Global.

Arianna married Michael Huffington in 1986 and moved to California. Eleven years later the couple got divorced. They have two daughters.

In 1997, she was nominated for a Primetime Emmy for the comedy talk show *Politically Incorrect*. She was named in *Forbes'* first-ever list of the 'Most Influential Women In Media' in 2009. In 2012, *The Huffington Post* became the first U.S. digital media business to win a Pulitzer Prize.

BILL GATES

BIRTH: October 28, 1955
Seattle, Washington, USA

Bill Gates, formally known as William Henry Gates III, founded the world's most significant software business, Microsoft. He is an American business tycoon, investor, author, humanitarian and one of the wealthiest men in the world.

Gates was born on October 28, 1955, in Seattle, Washington to William Henry Gates II and Mary Gates. His father was a lawyer, and his mother was a school teacher. When he was an elementary student, his teachers and principal knew that he had unique brain power. The principal advised his parents to enroll him in a private school. So, in 1967, Bill attended Lakeside School.

While there, he grew an interest in computing. At the age of thirteen, he wrote his first software on a school computer. In 1968, Gates began programming with Paul Allen, whom he'd met at school. At the age of seventeen, he formed a test called Traf-O-Data. He graduated from high school in 1973. During college exams, he scored 1590 out of 1600 on the SATs. He was a National Merit Scholar. In 1973, he entered Harvard College to study Law.

Gates was still engrossed in computers, and Allen wanted him to start a business. In 1975, Gates signed up for a job with MITS. MITS was the creator of the world's first personal computer. That year he founded Microsoft. They applied BASIC, a popular programming language for computers. This soon attained success, and they continued to develop the computing language for other systems.

In 1976, Gates and Allen registered the trademark 'Microsoft'. In 1979, Microsoft moved to Washington. After their success, they were approached by IBM in 1980. They signed a contract with IBM to write the software for their upcoming line of PCs. Microsoft bought the rights to the system called 'DOS' in 1981. Gates renamed it to MS-DOS. In 1985, Windows 1.0 was launched. Over the following years, Windows became a prominent software. About 90% of the market shares was taken by Windows. Gates flourished financially and in 1987, at the age of 31, he became the youngest billionaire ever. In 1989, Microsoft launched Microsoft Office. The system contained applications like Microsoft Word and Excel, which are regularly used worldwide now. The same year he founded Corbis. It was an application to organize collections of art and photography. It became the first collection of visual information in the world.

In 1995, Microsoft launched Windows 95. Gates introduced the Internet Explorer browser to the world.

At the age of 35, Gates became the world's richest man. Gates is also known as a great author and has published many books. In 1995, he released his book titled *The Road Ahead*. The story was about Gates' vision for the digital future. It became a *New York Times* bestseller. In 1999, he published another book called *Business @ the Speed of Thought*. Gates explained how business and technology are connected to each other in this book.

In the year 2000, Gates stepped down from the position of CEO. He took the title of Chairman until 2014. Currently, he plays the role of a technology advisor to support the CEO.

He began to spend more time in philanthropic pursuits. In 2000, Gates and his wife founded The Bill & Melinda Gates Foundation. They declared that about $1 billion would be given to help 20,000 young people for their college education. The foundation is known as one of the most important private foundations in the world. In 2006, he launched an eco-friendly project called TerraPower, whose aim is to provide the world with an affordable and environment-friendly form of nuclear energy.

Gates received many awards for his exceptional work including the Jefferson Award for Greatest Public Service in 2002. In 2010, he received the Bower Award for Business Leadership from The Franklin Institute. In 2015, Gates received India's third highest civilian honor, the Padma Bhushan.

In 1987, Gates met Melinda French for the first time. And on January 1, 1994, Melinda and Bill got married in Hawaii. They are the parents of three children.

ELON MUSK

BIRTH: June 28, 1971
Pretoria, South Africa

Elon Musk is a South African entrepreneur known for founding the ingenious Tesla Motors.

Elon Musk was born on June 28, 1971, in Pretoria, South Africa to Maye Musk and Errol Musk. His father was an electrical engineer. When his parents got divorced in 1980, Elon chose to live with his father in South Africa. At the age of nine, he got his first personal computer. He took an interest in programming and began learning it by himself. He finished a six-month course in just three days.

At the age of twelve, he sold his first self-made video game, 'Blastar'. After graduating from secondary school, he decided to leave home. In 1989, Elon moved to Canada. While staying there, he worked odd jobs like shoveling dirt in a boiling room.

At the age of eighteen, in 1989, he attended the Queen's University in Ontario for his under-graduate studies. In 1992, he was transferred to the University of Pennsylvania, obtaining a dual degree in Physics and Economics. He also holds a doctorate in Design from the Art Center College of Design and a doctorate in Aerospace Engineering from the University of Surrey. As a college student, Elon took up many internships. He worked as an intern in a bank, and a research and video game company.

Musk is an avid reader, and as a kid would read books for up to ten hours a day. He had an existential crisis while reading Douglas Adams' *The Hitchhiker's Guide to the Galaxy*. He learned his life's most valuable lesson after reading this book. He decided his life's mission was to save humanity. In 1995, he moved to California to attend Stanford University. He applied for a PhD in Physics but left the university after only two days.

Musk brainstormed his ideas with his brother, Kimbal Musk. He created his first IT company Zip2 in 1995. The biggest reason behind his success was the Internet, which was experiencing a period of growth and development. Nobody had tried to maneuver it to their own advantage before Musk's company.

In 1999, the company Zip2 was purchased by Compaq's Search engine, AltaVista. The same year Musk began working on an electronic payment method. His next business was called X.com. The company worked as an online bank. Musk soon faced competition in the form of a banking startup called Confinity.

In 2000, his company merged with Confinity to form PayPal, the biggest online payment portal in the world. In 2002, eBay bought PayPal. Musk stopped investing in Internet businesses and shifted his attention to his other interests like space engineering and energy sources.

In 2002, he invested in his third company, SpaceX. In 2001, he went to Russia to buy a rocket to send it to Mars. But his idea failed when he came to realize that rockets are extravagantly prized. Musk was still inspired by the idea of reducing space transportation costs to enable people to colonize Mars. In just seven years, the company designed the Falcon line of space launch vehicles and the Dragon line of multipurpose spacecraft. Musk's SpaceX received contracts from NASA to create a launch craft to deliver cargo to the International Space Station.

Musk is also known for designing Tesla Motors. Their first electric sports car is called the 'Tesla Roadster'. For his design of the Tesla Roadster, Musk received the Global Green Product Design Award.

He started Tesla Motors Company in 2003. In 2006, Musk invested in another company called SolarCity Corporation. SolarCity provides solar power systems for homes, businesses and governments. Today the company is one of the largest providers of solar energy and aims to fight global warming.

Musk is also involved in the development of rail systems. He received approval to build a Hyperloop from New York City to Washington D.C. By 2020, the first Hyperloop train will start running.

For changing the face of our future, Musk has been awarded several times. In 2010, Musk received the FAI Gold Space Medal for aerospace records. He was named 'Businessperson of the Year' by *Fortune* magazine. In 2016, he was included in the Forbes' list of 'The World's Most Powerful People'.

ESTÉE LAUDER

BIRTH: July 1, 1908
New York City, USA

DEATH: April 24, 2004 (aged 97)
New York City, USA

Estée Lauder was an American businesswoman and one of the wealthiest women entrepreneurs in America. She was the founder of Estée Lauder Companies Inc., one of the most famous cosmetic and fragrance companies in the world.

Estée Lauder was born as Josephine Esther Mentzer on July 1, 1908, in New York City to Max Mentzer and Rose Rosenthal. Her father owned a small hardware shop. Esther attended Newtown High School in Queens as a child. Due to her accent, her name was mistaken to be Estée while in school.

Estée learned the basics of business from her father. She would help her father in the shop after school. She learned the skill of making a sale, and giving special treatment to the customers during holidays like Christmas. As an adult, Lauder used the same tactics to get more customers for her own company.

Lauder decided at a very young age that she wanted to start her own business someday. Thus, she became an apprentice under her uncle, John Schotz. In 1914, after World War I, her uncle came to stay with the family. She described her uncle as "a magician and mentor." He was a chemist and had created four secret formulas for skin creams. Young Estée observed her uncle's work and realized her passion for cosmetics. She started selling her uncle's cosmetics to her friends and called them "jars of hope".

After graduating, she decided to pursue her love of business and venture into the makeup industry. She chose to work for her uncle and began to market his products. Her first client was a neighborhood salon she frequented. The owner of the salon had asked her the secret to her beautiful skin and Lauder introduced her uncle's cosmetics to the salon. The owner allowed Lauder to sell the products at the salon. She made significant sales and had soon earned a considerable amount of money.

In 1933, she worked restlessly to improve her uncle's creams. The one thing that made her cosmetics stand out was her use of natural ingredients. In just a few months, she had a trusted clientele, who were some of New York's most powerful people. The same year she founded Lauder Chemists. Her role was making the sales while her husband managed the finances. In 1944, she opened her first store in New York.

In 1946, she founded Estée Lauder Inc. with her husband. Initially, they only had four products. They had turned a restaurant into a factory.

Lauder cooked up the creams and oils through the nights. Customers appreciated her products for their high quality.

Success came to her in 1950. She traveled to different countries to spread the word about her brand. Her company was the first one to give free samples of cosmetics. She gained thousands of new customers in a very short time. Lauder called "free distribution" the only right way of running a business.

In 1953, she had a turning point in her career when she launched her Youth Dew product. It was her first fragrance. It became a great hit amongst women who couldn't afford expensive perfumes. The sale of Lauder's fragrance increased and turned her business into a multi-million dollar company. In 1964, she started to make products for men. She created a line of men's products called Aramis and Clinique.

Lauder became one of the wealthiest, self-made women in the world. Her products were being sold worldwide. She provided employment for many and inspired women all over the world to work towards their dreams. In 1985, she published her autobiography *Estée: A Success Story*.

Estée married Joseph Lauder on January 15, 1930. They had two sons.

In 2004, Estée Lauder received the Presidential Medal of Freedom. The same year this legendary woman died at the age of 97 in her home in New York.

HENRY FORD

BIRTH: July 30, 1863
Wayne, Michigan, USA

DEATH: April 7, 1947 (aged 83)
Dearborn, Michigan, USA

Henry Ford was the founder of the Ford Motor Company, one of the largest and longest-running car companies in America.

Henry Ford was born on July 30, 1863, in Michigan to William and Mary Ford. Since he was a young boy, Ford enjoyed tinkering with machines. Farm work and a job in a Detroit machine shop presented him with ample opportunities to experiment.

He practiced his skills on watches and repaired items for his friends and neighbors. Soon he gained the reputation of a watch repairman. After his mother died in 1876, he was devastated. He left home with a sixth-grade level education in 1879 and started to work in a factory in Detroit. He was an assistant machinist with James F. Flower & Bros. He was fired from his first job after just six days.

In 1882, before returning home, he began working for the Detroit Dry Dock Co. After coming back home, he started working on the family farm. He was also hired part-time as an engineer at Westinghouse Engine Company. Ford had never worked on steam engines before, however he immediately figured out the mechanics. Ford worked with them for two years. In 1884, he joined business school. He took a few courses at Goldsmith, Bryant & Stratton Business University in Detroit. It is considered to be the only formal training he ever received.

In 1891, his career took off. He learned about

electricity and its concepts while working as an engineer. A job at the Edison Illuminating Company in Detroit came as a major learning opportunity. Seeing Ford's hard work and determination, he was promoted in 1893 to chief engineer. By 1896, Ford built his first car. He created the first horseless carriage, the 'Quadricycle'. That year in August, Ford met Thomas Edison. Edison helped Ford to improve his design. He encouraged Ford and approved of his experimentation. Gradually they became great friends.

With Edison's help, Ford modified the model of his automobile and completed the second vehicle in 1898. After that, he dedicated himself solely to the business of automobiles. He left his job at Edison and decided to start his own company. He founded the Detroit Automobile Company in 1899. Ford's sponsors wanted fast profits, but his vehicles weren't of the best quality, and production was slow. The company produced only ten delivery trucks before closing.

It was later renamed to Cadillac Automobile Company.

In 1901, Ford rebuilt his reputation by racing. He drove his first race car, 'Sweepstakes', to victory. Finally, in 1903, the Ford Motor Company was born. In 1904, Henry Ford agreed with the idea of expanding and building Ford in Canada. A Ford plant opened in Ontario with seventeen workers. It was Ford's first international venture.

Ford transformed the way cars were made. He began the first automobile assembly line in 1913. Automobiles production became faster and cheaper than ever.

In 1915, he founded the Henry Ford Hospital. In 1916, Ford Trade School was established. The school taught the mechanisms of various machines. In 1926, Henry Ford built a Tri-Motor plane.

By 1928, Ford had assembled vehicles on six continents. The Model N was released in 1906. It became America's bestseller. The lightweight, inexpensive car included concepts that Ford has continued to develop over the years. He then began producing the Model T. It was durable, lightweight, easy to repair, and well-suited for bad roads. The demand was huge and kept growing rapidly. Soon, other companies also started to replicate this idea for their vehicles.

Ford married Clara Jane Bryant in 1888 and had one son, Edsel, with her. He died on April 7, 1947 at the age of 83 in his home. The cause of his death was a cerebral hemorrhage.

Ford was simply a hard worker who used his ideas to change the face of America. During his lifetime he was awarded the Franklin Institute's Elliott Cresson Medal in 1928.

HOWARD SCHULTZ

BIRTH: July 19, 1953
New York City, USA

oward Schultz is an American entrepreneur and the CEO of the Starbucks Coffee Company. Starbucks is the largest coffee store chain in the world.

Howard Schultz was born on July 19, 1953, in Brooklyn, New York to Fred and Elaine Schultz. He was born into a lower middle-class family. His father worked as a truck driver and his mother was a receptionist. When Howard was seven, his father lost his job because he broke his ankle. Due to this, Howard's family struggled financially.

But his parents wanted him to be educated so they enrolled him in Canarsie High School. He graduated in 1971. His only relief from his difficult life was sports. He was even awarded an athletic scholarship to the Northern Michigan University. Howard was the first person in his family to attend college. He received his Bachelor's degree in Communications in 1975.

After he graduated from college, he got a job at the Xerox Corporation as a sales representative. He worked with Xerox for four years. In 1979, he started to work at a Swedish company, Hamamaplast. He worked there as a general manager selling home appliances to customers. Schultz became curious about one of his customers who had purchased plastic cone filters and coffee machines in large quantities.

In 1981, he visited a coffee-bean shop called Starbucks Coffee Company in Seattle. He realized that the company was run by the same client. He was amazed by their knowledge and art of making coffee. Upon tasting the coffee, he was immediately impressed; it was better than anything he'd tried before. Inspired by their dedication, a business opportunity occurred to Schultz.

In 1982, he was offered the post of the Marketing Director at Starbucks. Next year, Schultz traveled to Italy; he noticed that every street had coffee bars that served as meeting places. Soon, he returned with tasteful recipes of lattes and cappuccinos, which increased Starbucks' sales. He also brought back the concept of creating cafes for social meetings. In the United States, socializing was mostly carried out in fast-food restaurants.

In 1985, Schultz proposed this idea to the CEO of Starbucks, to create a network of coffee houses. But the founder rejected his plans. Schultz however remained confident and resigned from the company. In 1985, he opened his coffee shop called Il Giornale meaning 'the daily'. His coffee shop was an instant success.

Schultz found out that the owners of Starbucks

were planning to sell the company. So, he secured a loan and bought Starbucks.

When Schultz visited Italy for the second time, he not only brought back photos and menus, but also videotapes in which he'd documented the Italian baristas in action. He showed the tapes to his employees to train them for better performance.

A major factor in Starbucks' success was how the company dealt with its employees. Schultz started a training program to groom his employees. He gave complete healthcare benefits to his full time and part-time employees. Schultz designed his coffee shops with the aim of encouraging customers to relax and converse. The menu started with a basic cup of coffee and later expanded to fancier coffee beverages such as espresso, cappuccino, café latte, iced coffee and café mocha.

Schultz experienced a massive growth through-out the 1990s. In 2000, he resigned as the CEO of Starbucks. However, he regained his position in 2007. He partnered with a French yogurt maker, and introduced a new Greek yogurt to the Starbucks menu.

Schultz is also involved in charitable work. In 1998, Starbucks came up with products to contribute to local literacy programs across America.

For his exceptional work as an entrepreneur, he was given the Israel 50th Anniversary Tribute Award in 1998. Schultz was awarded the National Leadership Award for his donations and educational efforts to battle AIDS in 1999. He received the International Distinguished Entrepreneur Award in 2004 and the FIRST Responsible Capitalism Award in 2007. He was named Fortune magazine's 'Businessperson of the Year' in 2011.

Schultz married Sheri Kersch, an interior designer in 1982. The couple have two children.

JACK MA

BIRTH: September 10, 1964
Hangzhou, China

Jack Ma is a Chinese entrepreneur who is the head of the Alibaba Group, including several of China's most famous websites.

Jack Ma, originally Ma Yun, was born on September 10th, 1964, in Hangzhou, China. His parents were traditional musicians and storytellers. As a kid, Jack always had an interest in learning the English language. In 1972, the former President of the United States of America, Richard Nixon, visited China. The president's visit progressed tourism in Jack's hometown. He wanted to make the most of this opportunity. He started visiting a hotel near his residence and slowly began giving guided tours to foreigners around the city for free. His motive was to spend more time with foreigners to gain a command over the English language. The nickname "Jack" was given to him by a tourist.

After he graduated from high school, he struggled to get into college. The Chinese college entrance exams are held only once a year, and Jack failed the entrance exams twice. He finally attended Hangzhou Teacher's Institute to pursue a Bachelor's degree in English. He graduated in 1988 and started to apply for jobs. However, he faced many rejections. Later, he got placed as an English lecturer at a local university. With his job, he continued his studies at the Beijing-based Cheung Kong Graduate School of Business (CKGSB). He graduated in 2006.

Jack learned about the existence of the Internet during the mid-90s. He started to see this new trend in technology as a business opportunity. He visited the United States in 1995 with his friends. It was one of his friends who taught him how to connect to websites for the first time. Jack's first online search was for beer but he noticed that no results came up from China. He knew then that starting a business in China, related to the Internet, would be valuable. After he came back from the States, he founded China Pages. It was one of China's first Internet companies. In just three years, the company made huge profits. Due to the success of his company, Jack was offered a job with the government. He worked as the head of the China International Electronic Commerce Center.

His big break came after resigning from the government office. In 1999, Jack founded a company called Alibaba along with seventeen other people. The company began in his apartment. Jack's Internet company Alibaba allowed customers to buy products directly from the website. The company received financial support from the very beginning, which significantly aided to its growth.

Their business expanded to around 240 different nations. In 2003, he started another e-commerce site called Taobao. It trended as the top website, grabbing the attention of Internet giants like eBay and Yahoo. In 2005, Yahoo invested billions of dollars in Alibaba. In 2007, Jack started two more companies. One was Alimama, an online company, and Alisoft, an Internet based software company.

With the success of his company Jack became one of the richest people in the world. Even though he is the wealthiest man in China, he remains grounded because of his humble beginnings. He still loves reading and writing kung fu fiction, playing poker, meditating, and practicing tai chi. In 2013, he stepped down from the post of CEO of Alibaba.

Jack is also passionate about the environment. He is a member of many environmental groups. In 2013, he became one of the members of the global board of The Nature Conservancy and spoke during the Clinton Global Initiative. He also donated several acres of land to a nature reserve in China. He is a member on the board of the World Economic Forum.

Jack is also the recipient of many awards and has appeared in many publications. In 2004, he was featured in the 'Top 10 Business Leaders of the Year' by China Central Television. In 2007, Jack was featured 'Businessperson of the Year' and one of the '25 Most Powerful Business People in Asia'. In 2015, at the Asian Awards ceremony he was awarded as the 'Entrepreneur of the Year'.

Jack married Zhang Ying in the late 1980s. His wife played a crucial role in helping him build his first business. The couple has two children.

JEFF BEZOS

BIRTH: January 12, 1964
Albuquerque, New Mexico

Jeff Bezos is an American entrepreneur and founder of the e-commerce giant, Amazon. Amazon is the most significant retailer on the World Wide Web and model for Internet sales.

Jeff Bezos, originally Jeffrey Preston, was born on January 12, 1964, in Albuquerque, New Mexico to Jacklyn Gise and Ted Jorgensen. His mother was very young when she got married. However, the marriage did not last very long, and his father married for a second time after which the family moved to Texas. Jeff attended the River Oaks Elementary School and later, Miami Palmetto Senior High School. While in school, he also joined the Student Science Training

Program at the University of Florida. In 1982, Bezos graduated from high school as the class valedictorian.

From a very young age, Bezos had an interest in mechanical work. As a kid, he used to dismantle his crib with a screwdriver. Bezos even made an electric alarm for his room. He would work on various science projects in his garage. As a high school student, he began his first business called the Dream Institute. It was started for young students to develop their creative thinking.

In 1982, he attended Princeton University. He planned to study physics there but changed his mind after he took a few classes. He decided to return to his love of computers and opted for Computer Science. Bezos was a bit of an all-rounder, so he not only got a summer job as an analyst in Norway in 1984, he was also the president of the Space Club at the University. In 1986, he graduated with two Bachelor of Science degrees.

After he graduated, Bezos joined Fitel. He

then joined D. E. Shaw & Co. in New York, in 1990. Because of his job, he traveled a lot between New York and London. He became the youngest vice president of the company. While he tried to come up with new investments for D.E. Shaw, he found that the World Wide Web was growing at a rapid rate. Bezos saw an opportunity to sell products online. To turn this idea into reality, he quit his job to focus entirely on his plan.

In 1995, he founded Amazon.com, an online bookstore. It was named after the South American river. They sold their first book in July 1995. In 1997, the company went public. Bezos paid zero tax for the products he sold through the Internet, which led him to earn huge profits from his business. Amazon quickly became the leading online bookstore. It was accessible 24 hours a day, the site was user-friendly and offered discounts to customers.

In 1998, Bezos started to expand Amazon beyond just selling books. Amazon's tag line 'Earth's Biggest Bookstore' was changed to

'Books, Music and More'. They added music and offered CDs and videos on sale. In 2002, Amazon introduced clothes as its next category. In 1999, Bezos invested in more online stores. Amazon is known as the first company to have a 1-Click system. The 1-Click system made the ordering process very easy. In 2000, Amazon changed their logo to a smile-shaped arrow pointing from 'a' to 'z' in the word 'amazon', to indicate that Amazon offered everything from A to Z.

In 2005, Bezos launched Amazon Prime, under which they cut down the shipping time for customers, leading to a massively positive response. Bezos revolutionized reading when he introduced the Kindle. It was a hand-held electronic reading device. In 2010, Amazon signed a deal with The Wylie Agency. It benefited both the authors and Amazon. Next, Bezos introduced Kindle Fire. They added a bright light to their e-reading devices which allowed users to read even in the dark. Amazon's competitor at the time was Netflix, a streaming service that started in 1997. In 2013, Bezos purchased *The Washington Post* and other publications.

When Bezos was young, he'd given a speech about livable space stations. He wanted to have a human presence in outer space. After the success of Amazon, Bezos started another company. In 2000, he founded an aerospace company named Blue Origin. With the help of advanced technologies, Blue Origin aims to offer space travel to the public.

For his exceptional work, Bezos was awarded an honorary doctorate in Science and Technology from Carnegie Mellon University in 2008. In 2012, Amazon was named as the 'Top Retailer of the Year' and received a gold medal.

Bezos married MacKenzie Tuttle in 1993. The couple got divorced in 2019 and has four children.

LARRY PAGE

BIRTH: March 26, 1973
East Lansing, Michigan, USA

Larry Page is an American entrepreneur and computer scientist. He is the co-founder of Google Inc.

Lawrence Page was born on March 26, 1973, in East Lansing, Michigan to Carl Page and Gloria. Both his parents were Computer Science graduates. His childhood home was full of computers and science journals. Hence, young Larry started to get attracted to technology.

At a very young age, he made a working ink-jet printer. At the age of twelve, he wanted to start his own company. In 1991, he graduated from the East Lansing High School. Later, he attended the

University of Michigan to pursue a Bachelor's degree in Computer Engineering. Larry became a part of the solar car team at the university. He continued his studies and obtained a Master's degree in Computer Science from Stanford University. There he met Sergey Brin. They both worked on a research project and soon became great friends. In 1996, they invented BackRub. It was run on the Stanford servers for many months. BackRub's primary goal was to provide the best and most important results on the web.

In 1997, Page and Brin decided to change the name of BackRub. They came up with the name Google after the term googol, a mathematical concept. They aimed to organize all of the world's information available on the web. In 1998, the company Google Inc. was established. Over the years, Google changed tremendously and introduced new updates. Google became available in French, German, Italian, Swedish, Finnish, Spanish, Portuguese, Dutch, Norwegian, and Danish. Yahoo soon became their partner. In 2001, Page stepped down as the CEO of the company. Eric Schmidt took over and became the new CEO of Google.

In 2004, Orkut was launched by Google. It was a social networking site. That year, Google became a great hit. After the success of Google, Page and Brin became millionaires. In 2005, Google released many more products and services like Google Maps, Mobile, Google Reader, and iGoogle. In 2006, Google purchased YouTube. They also added a new chat feature in Gmail, their emailing service.

In 2007, Google became partners with China Mobile and Salesforce.com. In 2008, Google Earth was released. In 2011, Larry Page became the CEO of Google again. To improve services for the public, he started to work day and night. At the end of 2012, the company had launched the first Chromebook laptop, Google Glass and many more products. Page experienced vocal cord paralysis in 2013. Due to this medical condition, his voice became softer. He faces difficulties while talking at a stretch.

Page used technological advancements and his intellect for philanthropic work as well. With Google apps, education was easily available to thousands of students in remote places like Kenya and Rwanda. An easy access to information helped the students to get basic education. Page created Google.org which contributes social issues and causes. He also supports causes like global hunger and poverty. He invests in Planetary Resources, an organization that mines asteroids. He began a children's book startup called Twigtale. In 2006, he started The Carl Victor Page Memorial Foundation.

In 2002, Page and Brin were named in the *MIT Technology Review* for being among the 'top 35 innovators in the world under the age of 35'. For his essential participation in science and technology, Page was awarded the prestigious Marconi Foundation Prize in 2004. For his achievements, Page was ranked number thirteen on the *Forbes'* '400 Richest Americans'; moreover, he ranked seventeenth on *Forbes'* '2013 Most Powerful People'.

Larry Page

Larry Page is a very private person. He married Lucinda Southworth, a scientist, in 2007. They have two kids.

MARK ZUCKERBERG

BIRTH: May 14, 1984
New York City, USA

Mark Zuckerberg is the developer of the globally used social networking website, Facebook.

Born on May 14, 1984, in White Plains, New York to Edward and Karen Zuckerberg, Mark's father is a dentist, and his mother is a psychiatrist. He has three siblings.

He studied at the Ardsley High School, New York, and later the Phillips Exeter Academy. From a very young age, he took an interest in astronomy, mathematics, physics, English classical literature and foreign languages. He was also a part of the fencing team. But most of all, he liked writing coding software. His father gifted him a computer and taught him Atari BASIC Programming.

Zuckerberg attended Mercy College at a very young age. He was taught Software Programming by the renowned professor David Newman. Zuckerberg developed a software called ZuckNet, and then, he and his friend created another software called Synapse Media Player. The software allowed users to make their own playlist. It gained a lot of media attention. Zuckerberg's Synapse Player was published on *Slashdot* and *PC Magazine*. He was already in demand for his products. While Microsoft offered one million dollars to buy off his software, AOL messenger application also tried to purchase it and offered him a job. However, Zuckerberg turned down both the offers.

In 2002, Zuckerberg graduated from Phillips Exeter Academy and moved to Harvard University. He studied Psychology and Computer Science.

During his college days, he was the go-to software developer on campus. In 2003, he built the software for CourseMatch—was a course selection program, and FaceMash—a rating app to compare physical features and attractiveness of people on campus. It was later revealed that Zuckerberg faced charges for creating FaceMash for "breaching security, violating copyrights and violating individual privacy." It also caught the attention of the university officials but he was allowed to remain as a student.

In 2004, Zuckerberg started The Facebook, a social networking site, with his friends. The site allowed users to create their own profiles, upload their photos, and communicate with other people.

He left Harvard in 2004 and focused on his company, The Facebook, later changing its name to Facebook. The website rose to fame by 2005, mostly due to the fact that Zuckerberg received enormous funding from Accel Partners. In just two years, Facebook became well-known all over the world. Zuckerberg had initially created this software for Harvard University students alone. However, Facebook later expanded to other educational institutions like Yale, Dartmouth and Stanford. In 2005, Facebook hit five million users. At the age of 22, in 2006, Zuckerberg turned away many big companies who wanted to acquire Facebook. He refused a billion-dollar offer from Yahoo and $15 billion from Microsoft.

In 2010, his journey was documented in the movie called *The Social Network*, starring Jesse Eisenberg. The film was based on the 2009 book *The Accidental Billionaires*, by Ben Mezrich. The movie received eight Academy Award nominations.

In 2010, Zuckerberg was named *Time* magazine's 'Person of the Year' and featured in *Vanity Fair* and *Forbes* as well.

Zuckerberg has utilized his generous earnings for charitable work. He invested millions of dollars to save the failing school system. In 2010, he signed The Giving Pledge. He pledged to donate at least half of his wealth to charity throughout his lifetime. He also donated to help out Ebola victims in West Africa.

At Harvard, Mark met Priscilla Chan. They dated for seven years and finally got married on May 19, 2012. The couple has two kids.

MARY KAY ASH

BIRTH: May 12, 1918
Hot Wells, Texas, USA

DEATH: November 22, 2001 (aged 83)
Dallas, Texas, USA

Mary Kay Ash was an American entrepreneur and the founder of the cosmetics giant Mary Kay Inc.

Mary Kay, originally Mary Kathlyn Wagner, was born on May 12, 1918, in Hot Wells, Texas to Edward Alexander Wagner and Lula Vember Hastings Wagner. Her father suffered from tuberculosis and spent most of his life in the hospital. It was her mother who took care of them. Mary had to look after the household from a very young age. It was her mother's constant motivation that kept her going all her life. She started her education at Dow Elementary School. She later moved to Reagan High School and graduated in 1934. She was an excellent student and won many awards. Due to her family's poor financial conditions, she could not attend university immediately. However, she earned enough money by herself, from her sales job, and enrolled at the University of Houston.

In 1939, she started working at Stanley Home Products. She used to go door to door to make sales. Ash was diagnosed with arthritis and yet she did not leave her job. However, she was very disappointed when she was not given the respect and due she deserved. Men who were less talented than her were promoted instead.

In 1952, she left her job and joined World Gift. She increased the company's profits and expanded the business to many states. She eventually became the director of the company.

After she faced gender discrimination once again, Ash left the job in 1962.

She decided to write a book based on her experiences and help other businesswomen. One day, she sat down at her kitchen table and made two lists. One list contained the good things she had seen in companies. The other, things she thought could be improved. When she combined the lists, Ash realized that she had created a marketing plan for a dream company. In 1963, she put this plan into action. She founded Beauty by Mary Kay. Ash met J. W. Heath who had developed a skincare formula that kept hands soft and wrinkle-free.

Ash bought the formula and used it as a product. Her golden rule for her company was faith first, family second and career third. To attract customers, she picked pink as her product's color. In just a few months, the company saw a profit.

The year 1964 was a stepping stone for Ash's

career. For the first time, she held a seminar which was more of a celebration. Eventually, it became a three-day annual event. In 1968, the company went public.

Ash also wrote her autobiography called *Mary Kay: The Success Story of America's Most Dynamic Businesswoman*. The book was a success, and millions of copies were translated into several languages. She worked on three more books, *Mary Kay on People Management*, *Mary Kay: You Can Have It All* and *Miracles Happen*.

Ash received many honors in her lifetime. Some of them are the Horatio Alger Distinguished American Citizen Award (1978), Dale Carnegie Leadership Award (1977) and Golden Plate Award by the American Academy of Achievement (1980). In 1996 she was inducted to the Business Hall of Fame. She was named the 'Most Outstanding Woman in Business' in the twentieth century in 2000.

Ash was also involved in charitable work.

She founded the Mary Kay Charitable Foundation in 1996. The foundation was started to support cancer patients, and to tackle domestic violence.

Ash married Ben Rogers at the young age of seventeen in 1935. The couple had three children. However, the marriage was not a happy one and they got divorced. In 1963, she married George Arthur Hallenbeck, a chemist. Unfortunately, he died of a heart attack just a few days into their marriage. Mary got married for the last time to Melville Jerome in 1966.

Gradually her whole family got involved in the business. Her two sons joined the company when it started and her daughter joined Mary Kay Cosmetics as one of the directors later on.

The same year, Ash suffered a stroke due to which she was unable to speak. Mary died on November 22, 2001, in her home.

MUKESH AMBANI

BIRTH: April 19, 1957
Aden, Yemen

Mukesh Ambani is an Indian business tycoon and the Chairman of Reliance Industries Limited (RIL). He is one of the wealthiest people in the world.

Mukesh Dhirubhai Ambani was born on April 19, 1957, in Aden, Yemen to Dhirubhai Ambani and Kokilaben Ambani. His father used to work at a firm in Yemen before he moved to Mumbai in 1958. For his education, Mukesh attended Hill Grange High School, Mumbai. After he completed his high school, he attended the Institute of Chemical Technology. He received a Bachelor's degree in Chemical Engineering. In 1980, he started studying Business Administration at Stanford University, but later quit college.

Mukesh wanted to assist his father in their family company, Reliance. He played a central role in growing the business legacy. Under his leadership, Reliance Industries expanded into sectors like petroleum refining, petrochemicals and gas exploration. He also set up Reliance Communication.

In 1980, Mukesh's father received a license from the government, over their competition like Tata, Birla, and others companies. In 1981, he formally joined Reliance Industries. His father had allotted him a polyester factory. Mukesh boosted the yarn manufacturing business of his father's company and spread it to the rural areas of India. Then, he doubled the business of petrochemicals. He was able to create many new world-class manufacturing facilities that raised Reliance's production volume.

The next industry he grew was Reliance Infocom Limited. It was one of his most notable achievements. It is now known as the largest and most complex information and communications technology company in the world.

Ambani experienced turmoil when his father passed away. The two Ambani brothers faced conflict over the ownership of Reliance. The crisis was settled by their mother, Kokilaben. Mukesh Ambani gained ownership of the oil, textile and refining businesses. Anil Ambani, his brother, took over the management and entertainment sectors of Reliance.

Reliance built the world's largest oil refinery company and became a thriving name in the oil and fuel industries. Today, Mukesh Ambani is one of the wealthiest persons in the world. Moreover, Reliance is the biggest commercial group in India.

However, Ambani also utilizes his enormous wealth to contribute to social welfare and charities.

His company offers a portion of their profits to different channels in the country. Sustainable development is a key area of his business, and their way of helping the environment. Reliance was voted among the top charitable organizations by a major Chinese media company.

For his exceptional work, Ambani has received many awards and featured in major publications. In 2004, he received the World Communication Award for the 'Most Influential Person'. In 2007, he was given the US–India Business Council "Global Vision" Award for leadership, and the same year the Chitralekha 'Person of the Year' Award by the Government of Gujarat. In 2010, he was named the 'Business Leader of the Year' at the IAA Leadership Awards.

In 2010, he received many honors like the Global Leadership Award and an honorary D.Sc. (Doctor of Science). In 2013, Ambani was declared as the 'Millennium Business Leader of the Decade' at the Indian Affairs India Leadership Conclave Awards. In 2014, he was ranked 36 on *Forbes'* list of the world's most powerful people. He was also awarded the Asia Society Leadership Award.

Mukesh married Nita Ambani in 1985. The couple have three children.

OPRAH WINFREY

BIRTH: January 29, 1954
Kosciusko, Mississippi, USA

Oprah Winfrey is an African-American entrepreneur, philanthropist, producer, actress, and television host. She is internationally famous for her TV show called *The Oprah Winfrey Show.*

Oprah Winfrey was born on January 29, 1954, in Mississippi, United States, to Vernon Winfrey and Vernita Lee. Her father was a coal miner and her mother a housemaid. As a child, Oprah loved playing with animals in her free time. She learned to read when she was only two. At the age of three, she gave her first recital at the local church.

Winfrey attended the East Nashville High School in Tennessee. She also worked for a local radio station as a newsreader. She won the Miss Black Tennessee Beauty Pageant in 1971. The same year she enrolled in Tennessee State University. There, Winfrey started to work in radio and television broadcasting in Nashville. She graduated from Tennessee State University with a degree in Speech and Performing Arts in 1973.

At the age of nineteen, Oprah worked as a news anchor for the local CBS television station. In 1976, she was a reporter and co-anchor for the ABC. In 1978, Oprah was hired as a show host for *People are Talking*. Oprah did wonders as a host, and her show was a hit. After she had worked there for eight years, she moved to Chicago. In 1983, she hosted a low-rated morning talk show called *AM Chicago*. Four years later, the show became a hit. In 1985, producers changed the show's name to *The Oprah Winfrey Show*. This show was a stepping stone in Oprah's career. Oprah won an Emmy award for the highest rated show in American history.

Millions of people watched the show on a regular basis. In 1990 Oprah made a few changes in the format of her show. She started focusing on more important topics like spirituality, meditation, celebrity interviews on social issues, and medical information. In 1993, she interviewed Michael Jackson for the first time. The episode became the most-watched interview ever.

She also tried her hand at acting with the movie *The Color Purple.* For her performance, she was nominated for an Academy Award for 'Best Supporting Actress'. After the movie's success, she was offered many roles in several films including in *Native Son* as Janet Thomason.

The year 1986 was an excellent year for Oprah. She started her own television company called Harpo Productions. The company produced movies and shows. With the assistance of her company, Oprah acted in the television mini-series *The Women of Brewster Place* in 1989 and its spin-off, *Brewster Place* in 1990.

Oprah was awarded the Woman of Achievement Award by the National Organization for Women in 1986. In 2000, she launched *O, The Oprah Magazine*. The magazine was the most successful startup magazine in the industry. She started another publication, *O at Home*, in 2004. In 2005, she was a guest on the *Late Show with David Letterman*. In 2006, she was a voice artist for the animated film called *Charlotte's Web*, and started Oprah Radio. She again gave voice to the *Bee Movie* in 2007 and *The Princess and the Frog* in 2009. In 2011, Oprah began her own network called OWN: Oprah Winfrey Network. It was a joint venture with the Discovery Health channel. The first television show that aired on OWN was *Greenleaf*, with Oprah as a part of the cast. In 2017, Oprah joined the news magazine *60 Minutes*.

Oprah was the wealthiest African-American of the twentieth century, according to *Forbes*, and the world's first black billionaire. *Life* magazine called her the most influential woman of her generation.

Oprah has been deeply involved in philanthropic work throughout her life. In 1998, Oprah formed the Angel Network which encourages people to engage in charitable and volunteer work. She raised millions for girls' education in South Africa and the victims of hurricane Katrina.

Oprah also founded the Better Lives Foundation in 2008. The organization fights for children's rights. She was awarded by the Academy of Television Arts & Sciences. In 2013, Oprah received the Presidential Medal of Freedom. In 2018, she won the Golden Globe Lifetime Achievement Award.

PETER JONES

BIRTH: March 18, 1966
Berkshire, England

Peter David Jones is a British entrepreneur and businessman who gave a new definition to the word ambition. At present, he is the CEO of some major businesses, and is a famous television personality.

Peter Jones was born on March 18, 1966, in Berkshire, England. Peter's father owned a small business. Both his parents worked full-time to provide the family with as much as they could. Peter always looked up to his father. Even as a child Peter loved visiting his father's office and sitting in the big chair, imagining yielding all the power. Peter believed that one day he would be a multi-millionaire.

For his education Peter attended a couple of private schools and then studied at Desborough College. For his high school education, he mainly went to Windsor Boys' School. He developed an interest in Economics and tennis. He was good at tennis, so he spoke to his English teacher John Woodward, who owned a summer tennis school. Peter learned the game there. His teacher also taught him the art of running a business. Peter passed the Lawn Tennis Association's coaching exam. After he cleared the exam, he set up his own tennis coaching school and became a coach. By the time he graduated from school he had become an expert in the sport, and also economics.

Jones started his career very early on. In his twenties, he had founded a company that made and sold computers. His business was successful. Within a year he was able to own a beautiful house, an expensive car and had plenty of money at his disposal. However, he made some mistakes due to which his business failed. He also started a restaurant, but that didn't do well either. Jones lost all his money. To pay the bills he began to work for the company Siemens Nixdorf. It was a large telecommunications company.

In 1998, he founded the Phones International Group and sold mobile phones to different clients. This business put him back on top. He earned millions in the first year itself. From 2004-08, Peter expanded his business and opened three more companies, Generation Telecom, Celsius, and the online company Wines4Business.com. He invested his money in more than twenty companies.

The year 2005 was the best year in Jones' career. He became a well-recognized television star after his appearance as a judge on the British TV show *Dragons' Den*. The concept of the show was for the contestants to pitch and sell their business plans to a team of judges. Jones went on to work in TV shows like *American Inventor, James Corden's World Cup Live, The Magicians, ITV Celebrity Juice*, and *Top Gear*'s "Star in a Reasonably Priced Car" segment. In 2006, he produced *Tycoon*, a television series broadcast by the ITV network. Jones also owns a production company called Peter Jones TV.

He also started an academy called the Peter Jones Enterprise Academy. There he taught how to run a business to aspiring entrepreneurs.

Jones has also made many sound property investments. In 2008, he cleared the Business Studies A-level exam. Jones currently invests in more than forty businesses including publishing, new media, television, entertainment and food products.

Jones also utilizes his money for good causes. He founded the Peter Jones Foundation in 2005. He raised awareness about the importance of education. His foundation aims to encourage and provide education to young kids.

For his exceptional work, Jones has been honored many times. He was presented the Emerging Entrepreneur of the Year Award by Ernst & Young. In 2009, he was given the title of Commander of the Order of the British Empire by the government.

Peter Jones was married to Caroline. The couple had a daughter and a son. However, the marriage did not last long. Since 1997, Jones has been in a relationship with Tara Capp. The couple has three children.

Jones proved to the world that absolute dedication can overcome any obstacle in life.

PHIL KNIGHT

BIRTH: February 24, 1938
Oregon, USA

Phil Knight is the co-founder of Nike Inc., one of the world's largest suppliers of athletic shoes and apparel. He was named as the 'Most Powerful Person in Sports' by *Sports Illustrated*, although he is neither a sportsman nor the owner of a sports team.

Philip Hampson Knight was born on February 24, 1938, in Portland, Oregon to William W. Knight and Lota. His father was a lawyer and newspaper publisher. For his education, Philip attended Cleveland High School. He graduated from the University of Oregon with a Journalism degree in 1959. He served in the army for a year and then pursued an MBA degree at Stanford.

Three major events shaped Knight's future and led him to the ownership of Nike. The first was meeting his track team coach, Bowerman, a legendary track coach and former Olympian. The second major event was attending Business School at Stanford University. While he worked on his Master's degree, he came up with the first blueprint for what would eventually become the world's number one athletic shoe company. He wrote his term paper on how to start a small sports shoes business and developed a plan to create a cheaper but better-quality running shoe.

The third major event was when he visited Japan which shaped his future brand. He discovered the Tiger running shoe brand distributed by Onitsuka Co. Knight was amazed at how the company created high quality and low-cost shoes. He reached out to make a distribution deal with the company and convinced them that they had a market in the U.S. The first shipment of the shoes arrived in 1963, and Knight established the company Blue Ribbon Sports with Bowerman.

Both of them invested a few hundred dollars

to start their first company. Knight purchased several pairs of Tiger running shoes and began to sell them out of his car at high school track meets throughout the Pacific Northwest.

The company struggled in its initial days. Knight needed a regular income, so he continued to work as an accountant. He also taught at Portland State University. Over the next few years, they opened retail stores in Santa Monica, California and Oregon. The company started to pick up its performance, and by the late 1960s they were generating good profits.

A friend of Knight's, Jeff Johnson, suggested the name "Nike". It was inspired by the Greek goddess of victory. A graphic design student, Carolyn Davidson, designed the "swoosh" logo for them. In 1972, Blue Ribbon launched its Nike line. Knight was the first person to use a waffle sole in his products which made the shoes incredibly lightweight.

To come up with the world's best athletic shoes, Knight focused on the athletes. As a former athlete, he wanted to design products that the world's top athletes would love to use. Nike's new model, called the 'Cortez', was launched during the 1972 Olympics. It proved to be a highly profitable design. People saw their favorite sports stars wearing Nike which developed a buzz around the brand. In 1980, Nike became the leading athletic shoe brand. Due to the success of Nike, many famous sportspersons actively started to promote the brand. This list included the likes of Michael Jordan and Tiger Woods. In 1986, Nike's total sales were in billions of dollars. Nike outdid Adidas to become the number one shoemaker worldwide.

In 1990, Knight was criticized for not having a black president or any black board members in the company. Knight soon hired the first black board member. However, he was also criticized by human rights activists. He was accused of unfair treatment towards Asian workers who were paid meager wages. In the midst of all the negative publicity, Nike sales remained strong.

Knight also branched out into hockey, golf, and soccer clothing. Features like Nike's "Just Do It" tag line and images of Michael Jordan jumping in the air, made Nike the top brand in the industry.

Knight also actively participates in charitable work to help the society. He donated millions, one of the largest individual donations, to the Stanford Graduate School of Business. In 2008, he donated to the OHSU Knight Cancer Institute.

RATAN TATA

BIRTH: December 28, 1937
Mumbai, India

Ratan Tata is an Indian industrialist, investor, philanthropist, and the former chairman of Tata Sons.

Ratan Naval Tata was born on December 28, 1937, in Bombay, India to Naval Tata and Sonoo. After his parents separated, Ratan and his brother were brought up by their grandmother. He was brought up in a wealthy, famous Parsi family, who'd been in the business since the British rule in India.

For his education, Ratan attended Campion School, Cathedral School and then John Connon

School. He graduated from Cornell University in 1962 with a degree in Architecture and Structural Engineering. He continued his education with an Advanced Management Program at Harvard Business School in 1975. He was in the Alpha Sigma Phi fraternity, a prestigious club in the college.

The start of his career was in 1962. On his return, he joined the family business. He even turned down a job offer from IBM. As a child, he was always interested in cars and their functioning. Soon he started working as an ordinary employee in Tata Steel. His job was to shovel stones and work with the furnaces. It was a difficult task, but he gained knowledge and respect for his family business.

Ratan worked as a blue-collar employee till 1971. Given his hard work, he was promoted to the position of director. During this period, the National Radio and Electronics company was in a terrible state. However, soon after Ratan Tata joined the company, he made remarkable progress. In 1977, he moved to Empress Mills, which is a part of the Tata Group. He came up with a plan to make the mill business profitable. However, other Tata executives rejected it. Soon the mill was shut down. So Ratan was moved to Tata Industries.

In 1991, Ratan became the new chairman of the Tata Group of companies. Many people questioned his ability to run the business, however, he succeeded and improved the financial state of Tata Industries. Under his direction, Tata Group acquired major divisions like Tetley, Jaguar, Land Rover and Corus. He turned the company into a worldwide business. Tata became all the more famous when he introduced the world's cheapest car, the Tata Nano, in 2008.

On his 75th birthday, he resigned from the post of chairman of the Tata Group. Although he still keeps an eye on the new businesses and actively takes part in the decisions. Tata is also a member of the advisory board of Mitsubishi

Corporation, JP Morgan Chase, the American International Group, and Booz Allen Hamilton.

Ratan Tata put his hard work and determination to use for charities as well. Most of his shares are forwarded to charities. One of his primary goals is to improve the quality of life for Indians. He became a member of the Prime Minister's Council on Trade and Industry. He served on the advisory board of the RAND Center for Asia Pacific Policy. He is also an active participant in India's AIDS program.

Tata was called 'India's Most Respected Business Leader' by *Forbes*. The Indian government requested Tata to save the airlines Air India from sinking. Tata even successfully managed to make Air India profitable.

Ratan Tata is a renowned personality and has received many awards and recognition across the world. He received the Padma Bhushan in 2000. He also received the Padma Vibhushan in 2008. Tata was knighted in 2009. He won the Lifetime Achievement Award in 2012. He received an

Honorary Doctor of Law degree from York University, Canada in 2014.

Tata was honored as the 26th Robert S. Hatfield Fellow in Economic Education. It's the highest honor at Cornell University. He also got a doctorate from the London School of Economics. Tata was ranked amongst the '25 Most Powerful People in Business' by *Fortune* magazine in 2007.

Ratan Tata never got married. He is a very private person and lives a low-profile lifestyle. He lives in a simple house in Mumbai and drives around in a Tata sedan. He played a major role in raising the standard of living of the common man in India. Ratan Tata has made his country incredibly proud.

RAY KROC

BIRTH: October 5, 1902
Illinois, USA

DEATH: January 14, 1984 (aged 81)
California, USA

Ray Kroc was an American entrepreneur and the genius behind the world's most famous fast-food chain restaurant, McDonald's.

Raymond Albert Kroc was born on October 5, 1902, in Oak Park to Alois Louis Kroc and Rosemary. His father worked in the telegraph company, and his mother was a piano teacher. Ray attended Lincoln School in Oak Park. He was a confident boy and excelled in his studies.

Ray started to work at a very young age. While in grammar school he started a lemonade stand in front of his house. This was his first job in the food industry. He also worked in a grocery store.

At the age of fourteen, Ray opened a music store with his friend. The store was called the Ray Kroc Music Emporium. He sold sheet music while he played the piano. However, the store shut down in just a few months. At the age of fifteen, he served in the First World War as a Red Cross ambulance driver. After he finished his service, he returned to Chicago. He tried his luck at various jobs like being a paper cup salesman, a jazz musician, a pianist, a radio DJ and a band member.

Kroc started his career in 1919. He joined the American Stock Exchange in New York. His job was to read ticker tapes and translate symbols. At the age of 21, he took up a job as a salesperson for Lily-Tulip Cup Co. Kroc was young, ambitious and worked for long hours. He traveled a lot to sell paper cups. Kroc soon became the company's top salesperson.

That year he met Earl Prince. Earl had invented

the shake-mixing machine called Multimixer. Kroc knew Multimixer had great potential and got the marketing rights for the product. Kroc quit the Lily Tulip Paper Cup Company, after working there for sixteen years. In the 1940s, Kroc sold Multimixers around the country.

Shortly after, the demand for these mixers went down and Kroc lost dozens of his customers. However, at that time he received an order of eight machines from a small restaurant. He was curious about the order, so he went to see for himself what kind of restaurant needed to make those many milkshakes at a time. It was a small hamburger stand run by two brothers. Kroc was amazed by the McDonald brothers' restaurant. It was a self-service restaurant with no indoor seating, and the menu was limited to cheeseburgers, hamburgers, fries, drinks, and milkshakes. He saw that the customers got their meals in less than a minute. The preparation and sale of such a large volume of food in a short time amazed Kroc.

He started to dream of a McDonald's chain.

He approached the McDonald brothers but they were not interested in continuing this business. So, Kroc offered to do it for them. The brothers agreed and gave Kroc the rights to a franchise.

The same year, Kroc opened his first restaurant in Illinois, and by the end of the year two more. He used the McDonald brothers' method, making sure the taste was consistent across restaurants, and paid special attention to cleanliness. Then, Kroc met Harry Sonneborn, a financial genius. Sonneborn showed him how to earn money by selling real estate. To make more profit, Kroc opened another company that would buy or rent land, on which the McDonald's restaurants stood.

In 1950, Kroc and the McDonald brothers were involved in a dispute over changes in the restaurant. Therefore, in 1961, Kroc bought the McDonald's brand entirely. However, the brothers refused to give the original McDonald's restaurant in San Bernardino. So, Kroc opened a brand-new McDonald's one block away from the original store, now named 'The Big M,' to put them out of business. By 1965 he had opened several restaurants spanning 44 states.

Kroc was known as the 'King of the Hamburger' in the fast food industry. Kroc received the Horatio Alger Award for his dedication and honesty in 1972. He once said, "The two most important requirements for major success are: first, being in the right place at the right time, and second, doing something about it."

Kroc married thrice. He died of heart failure in California on January 14, 1984.

RUPERT MURDOCH

BIRTH: March 11, 1931
Melbourne, Australia

Rupert Murdoch is a famous Australian-born American newspaper publisher and media entrepreneur. He built a powerful international media empire and changed the journalism scene all over the world.

Keith Rupert Murdoch was born on March 11, 1931, in Melbourne, Australia to Keith and Elisabeth Joy Greene. His father was a well-known Australian journalist who owned some local and regional newspapers like the *Herald* and the *Courier-Mail*. Rupert grew up in a house full of journalists and was prepared to make a career in publishing from a very young age.

For his education, he went to Geelong Grammar School. As a student, he worked as an editor for various school journals like *The Corian* and *Revived*. Rupert even worked part-time at the *Melbourne Herald*. After he graduated in 1949, he continued his studies and went to Worcester College, University of Oxford. He showcased his talent for writing when he was in college. He was the head of Oxford Student Publications Limited.

After he got his Master's degree, he started to work with the *Daily Express* as an editor. His life changed significantly after the death of his father. He took control of his father's media company called News Limited. One of its newspapers, *Adelaide News*, achieved the highest circulation after the young man took over. Due to his success, in 1960, the company managed to buy the *Sunday Times* in Perth and *The Daily Mirror* in Sydney. In 1964, he started a national newspaper, *The*

Australian. It was the first newspaper started in Canberra, Australia. Around 1969, Murdoch moved to the British newspaper industry. He bought *News of the World*, the UK's highest selling newspaper. In 1969, Murdoch bought *The Sun*, a broadsheet newspaper. Its format was changed to a tabloid after it gained some success.

In 1972, Murdoch gained ownership of more newspapers. One was Sydney's *Daily Telegraph*. Another one was the *San Antonio Express-News*. In 1973, Murdoch expanded to the American market. The next year he launched a new tabloid called *Star*. He expanded further and started the *New York Post* in 1976.

In 1979, Murdoch founded News Corporation and served as the chairman. The year 1981 was a fruitful year for Murdoch. He took over a few other publications, like the eminent British newspaper, *The Times*.

Murdoch was recognized for his political views which he included in all his newspapers. In 1985,

Murdoch gained control of 20th Century Fox Film. He started TV stations under his company News Corporation. Over the next decade, he made Fox network the fourth national TV network in the U.S. He took control of Fox News, Fox Sports, and FX. In the next three years, he bought American publishers Harper & Row, and Collins. Later, he joined the two to form HarperCollins. He took control of *The Herald* and *The Weekly Times* as well.

His broadcasting business was also booming. In 1989, he launched Sky television in the UK. The company managed the UK TV market with millions of subscribers. After he had his foot in the USA and UK markets, he began to eye the Asian media market. In 1993, he bought StarTv in Asia. It helped him to spread news and other programs to countries like India and Japan.

In 1995, he started a news website called *The Weekly Standard*. The Fox Network was also introduced in Australia by News Corp. In 1996, Murdoch launched an all-day Fox News channel in the U.S. In 1999, he bought the Australian music company Mushroom Records to launch the Festival Mushroom Records. News Corp soon became a multi-billion-dollar company.

In 2007, Murdoch made the headlines when he purchased *The Wall Street Journal,* for $5 billion. The deal made Murdoch the most intimidating figure in the business of news coverage worldwide. In 2014, Murdoch announced that two of his sons would take over the leadership roles in the company. Murdoch's younger son, James, is the CEO of most of the companies.

SIR RICHARD BRANSON

BIRTH: July 18, 1950
Surrey, England

Sir Richard Branson is an English entrepreneur, investor and the founder of the Virgin Group.

Sir Richard Branson was born on July 18, 1950, in Blackheath, London to the lawyer Edward James Branson and Eve Huntley Branson. He received his early education from Scaitcliffe School and then attended Stowe School at the age of sixteen. He was dyslexic and thus, academically weak.

At Stowe School, the library was his shelter. He would spend his afternoons writing. In his school days, he met Jonathan Holland-Gems who nurtured the passion of writing in Richard. He started to become proactive in school activities. Soon, he participated in school essay competitions and won many. He began his first magazine while he was still a student. At the age of sixteen, he dropped out of high school.

In 1973, he launched a record label called Virgin Records. The first artist under the label was Mike Oldfield, who recorded the song "Tubular Bells". The song sold millions of copies. Eventually, Virgin Records became one of the top record companies in the world. Branson expanded his creative efforts and began his own travel company called the Voyager Group in 1980.

In 1984, he launched Virgin Atlantic Airways and Virgin Cargo. In 1992, he sold Virgin Records to fund Virgin Atlantic. It was a great success as the airline always went the extra mile to satisfy its customers. He introduced additional features like in-flight messages, video screens in every class, and free ice cream during movies.

Branson loved sports and adventure, so he took

part in the Virgin Atlantic challenge. He attempted the fastest Atlantic crossing. However, his boat turned and was later recovered by a helicopter. He still took part in the second challenge in 1986 and broke the record by two hours.

In 1987, he started the Virgin Airship and Balloon Co. The same year, Branson became the first person to cross the Atlantic Ocean in a hot air balloon. In 1994, he founded Virgin Radio. After having sold Virgin Records for one billion dollars, he knew he wanted to stay in the music business. So, in 1996, he started a second record company, V2.

In 2004, Branson started a space tourism company called Virgin Galactic. In 2012, he announced the orbital space launch vehicle called 'LauncherOne'. In 2013, he did a test-launch for SpaceShipTwo. The launch was a great success. Branson now plans to debut his Virgin cruise ships by 2020. The ship will hold a thousand guests and crew members.

His other significant investments include Virgin Fuels (2006). The company's goal is to produce clean fuel in the future. In 2007, Branson launched the Virgin Health Bank to store stem cells for the future. In 2010, the company launched Virgin Racing. It was their formula one team. The same year he started Virgin Produced. The company produces their own TV shows and films.

Branson is also a great author. He published an autobiography, *Losing My Virginity*, in 1998, that highlights his story from rags to riches. The book became a bestseller.

In 2007, he formed Elders with the support of Nelson Mandela. The organization is an independent group of global leaders. These leaders work together for peace and human rights. In 2011, Branson served as one of the members in the Global Commission on Drug Policy.

Branson's multitude of achievements and businesses all over the world are hard to believe. He always tells his followers "to dream big and live up to it."

Over the years of life, he has received many honors like the Tony Jannus Award and the German Media prize, to name a few. In 2007, for his charitable work, he was given the Citizen of the World award. For his contribution to space transport systems, he received the ISTA prize. In 2014, he was honored with the Oslo Business for Peace Award.

STEVE JOBS

BIRTH: February 24, 1955
San Francisco, California, USA

DEATH: October 5, 2011 (aged 56)
Palo Alto, California, USA

Steve Jobs was a technology visionary best known as the co-founder, chairman, and CEO of Apple Inc. He is known as the 'Father of the Digital World'.

Steven Paul Jobs was born on February 24, 1955 in San Francisco, to Abdulfattah Jandali and Joanne Schieble who gave him up for adoption. Paul and Clara Jobs adopted him. His family moved to California when he was five years old.

Jobs was exposed to the world of mechanics at a very young age. He used to rebuild electronic devices in his family's garage. Steve's father taught him how to build electronics such as radios and televisions. His mother home-schooled him. In 1968, young Steve called up Bill Hewlett to get a summer job at the HP factory. The next year Steve became friends with Steve Wozniak, with whom he shared a love of electronics and music. After he passed high school, he attended Reed College in 1972. But, he dropped out of college in just six months. Instead he pursued creative classes and calligraphy to learn artistic letter writing.

Jobs' first job was with Atari Inc. in Los Gatos, California. He worked as a video game designer at the company until 1974 and created a circuit board for video games.

In 1976, Jobs and Wozniak founded the Apple Computer Company. They sold circuit boards to their clients. The two of them invented the Apple I computer. The same year, Wozniak and Jobs introduced the early Apple I board at the Homebrew Computer Club. It was called the digital 'Blue Box' which allowed free long distance calls.

In 1977, Mike Scott became the CEO of Apple. Wozniak left HP and joined Apple full time. In the West Coast Computer Faire in 1977, Apple introduced their Apple II model to the public. The Apple II became one of the world's first personal computers. In 1980, they launched Apple III, but it was a failure. The same year, Apple went public and became a million-dollar company.

In 1981, IBM launched the IBM PC which quickly became a threat to Apple's future. So, in 1984, the Macintosh software was launched at Apple's annual meeting.

In 1985, Jobs left Apple due to disagreements between him and the CEO. He started his own company called NeXT Inc. In 1986, he invested in the newly independent Pixar Animation Studios and became a Chairman. In 1988, NeXT and IBM formed a partnership. In 1991, Pixar signed a deal with Disney and created the computer-animated film *Toy Story*. The movie was released in 1995, the same year Jobs became President & CEO of

Pixar. Following the success of *Toy Story*, Jobs became a billionaire.

In 1997, Jobs joined Apple as the CEO again. He rebuilt the damaged brand image of Apple. In 1998, Apple's iMac computer was introduced. Jobs became the permanent CEO of Apple in 2000. In 2001, he launched the iPod, iTunes digital music software, and iTunes Store. It was an instant success. Pixar was also on the path to success. In 2003, Pixar released another movie called *Finding Nemo*. The movie won the 'Best Animated Feature' Academy Award. In 2005, Disney bought Pixar, and Jobs still remained the largest shareholder in the company.

In 2007, Steve released a new product called the iPhone. It was the first touch-screen phone. It was named the 'Invention of the Year' by *Time*. In 2010, he introduced the iPad as, "the biggest thing Apple ever did."

Jobs received several awards for his revolutionary inventions in the field of technology.

He won the National Medal of Technology and the Jefferson Award for Public Service. He was inducted to the California Hall of Fame in 2007. He was named the most powerful person in business and 'CEO of the Decade' by *Fortune* magazine. Jobs was posthumously awarded the Grammy Trustees Award in 2012 for the iPod, which undoubtedly had a significant impact on the music industry.

In August 2011, Jobs resigned as the CEO of Apple. Steve Jobs died shortly after on October 5, 2011, at the age of 56 at home, surrounded by family. California Governor Jerry Brown declared October 16 as 'Steve Jobs Day' in his honor.

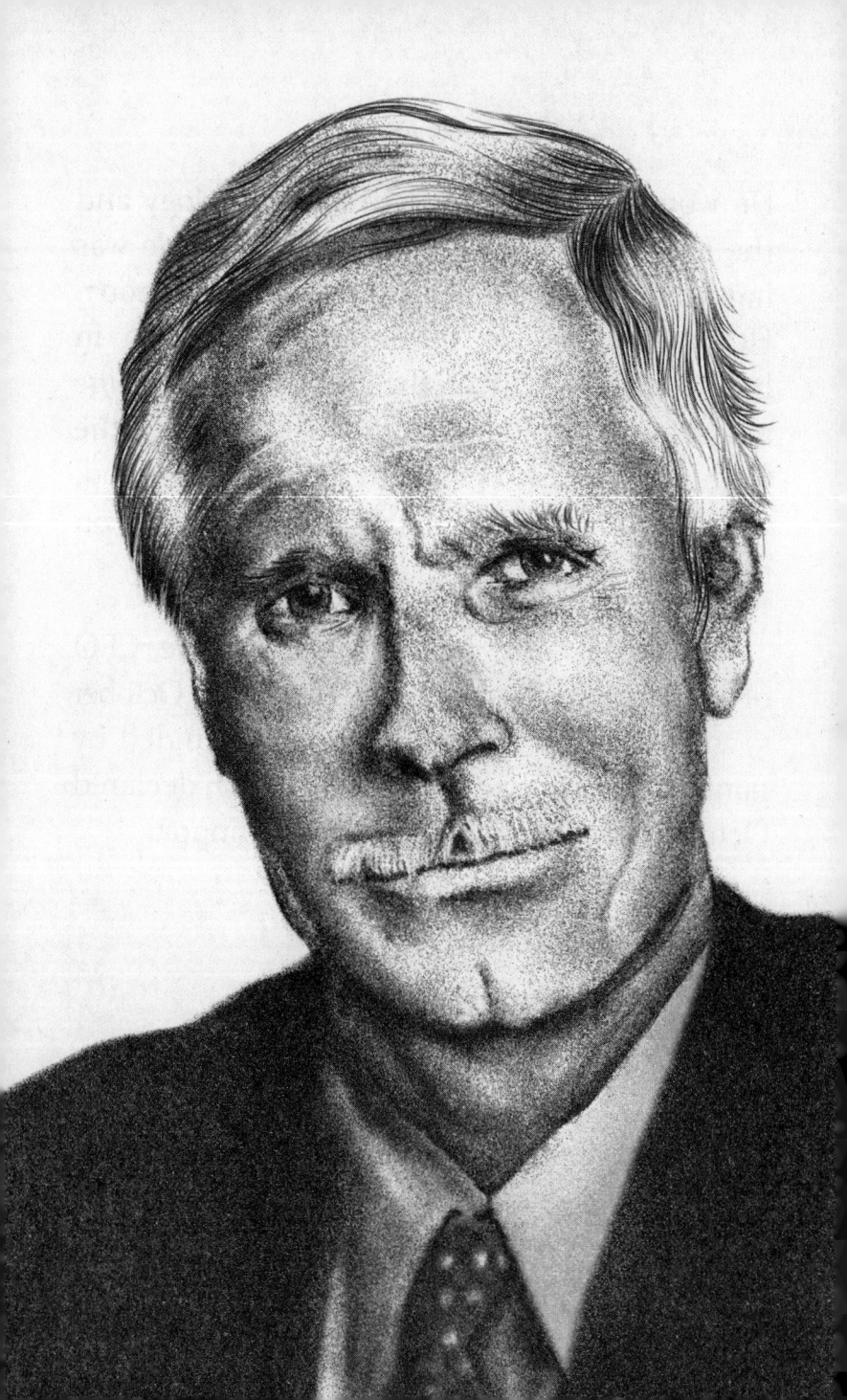

TED TURNER

BIRTH: November 19, 1938
Ohio, USA

Ted Turner is an American broadcasting entrepreneur, humanitarian, sportsman and nature lover. He is a media tycoon and the founder of the first ever 24-hour cable news network, 'CNN'.

Ted Turner, also known as Robert Edward, was born on November 19, 1938, to Robert Edward Turner Jr. and Florence. His father was a successful businessman who owned an advertising company called Turner Advertising.

Ted suffered from bipolar disorder and thus, had a tough childhood. He attended a boarding school in Ohio. After he completed his high school education, he went to Brown University in 1956 to study Economics. However, he was suspended from the University in 1959.

Turner soon joined his father's business, working as an assistant manager for Turner Advertising. The year 1963 was a low point for Turner. His father committed suicide, forced by a failing business and horrible finances. Turner was only 24 when he became the president of Turner Advertising. He changed the company's name to Turner Communication. In 1976, he launched the Turner Broadcasting System Superstation. The same year, the Superstation started broad-casting old movies, comedy shows, cartoons and sports specials. Turner's company was the first to use satellite technology and nationally broadcast shows to their subscribers.

The year 1980 was productive for Turner. He turned all his channels into Superstations. Over the years, Turner worked hard to create two highly successful and winning cable television networks: CNN (Cable News Network) and TNT (Turner Network Television). In 1980, CNN was formally launched and became the first 24-hour, all-news network in the USA. The channel covered all types of news, and within five years it started to make profits. With its raging success, it was extended to CNN Radio and CNN International. He launched other channels like Turner Entertainment Co. in 1986, Cartoon Network in 1992 and Turner Classic Movies in 1994.

His next big success was the launch of Turner Network Television (TNT) in 1988. The first show aired on the network was *Gone with the Wind*. The channel also began telecasting sports events like pro-wrestling and gained double the amount of audience. By the end of the 1980s, Turner became the most significant supplier of cable systems. It made him a billionaire. Turner was listed by *Forbes* magazine as one of the '400 Richest Americans' for several years.

With the launch of Cartoon Network in 1992,

Turner released the cartoon libraries of *Looney Tunes* and other classic cartoon characters. In 1994, the Turner Classic Movie (TCM) channel was released.

Turner made the most significant deal for the company with Time Warner in 1996. Time Warner was a newspaper, website, and TV giant at the time. The CEO of Time Warner was extremely interested in acquiring the Turner Broadcasting company. The company became a subsidiary of Time Warner upon acquisition. The deal was beneficial for both parties. The second, more debatable, agreement was between Turner and Fox network. However, the deal fell through. In 2000, AOL and Time Warner became one company. In 2003, Turner quit as the vice chairman, losing billions of dollars upon resignation.

Turner had been interested in sports from a very young age and was an extra-curricular enthusiast. Sailing was among these interests. In the 1970s, he participated in world championships and raced all over the globe. He participated in the race for America's Cup in 1974 but lost. In 1977, he competed once again with a yacht called "Courageous", and won the cup that year. Again in 1979, he entered the UK's Fastnet race with a newer boat called the "Tenacious" which came first amongst all the ships that competed in one of the deadliest ocean races in history.

Apart from being a sports enthusiast, Turner actively supports environment-related causes. He founded the Better World Society in 1985 and Turner Foundation in 1990. He also played an active role in the United Nations Association by donating billions of dollars to the UN. Turner received the Albert Schweitzer Gold Medal for humanitarianism in 2001.

WALT DISNEY

BIRTH: *December 5, 1901*
Illinois, USA

DEATH: *December 15, 1966 (aged 65)*
California, USA

Walt Disney was a television producer and showman. He was the ingenious creator of classic cartoon characters like Mickey Mouse and Donald Duck, and of the "happiest place on Earth", Disneyland.

Walter Elias "Walt" Disney was born on December 5, 1901, in Chicago, Illinois to Elias Disney and Flora Call Disney. His father was Irish-Canadian and his mother was German-American. When he was only four, his family shifted to Missouri.

Walt began to take an interest in drawing and painting from a very young age. He would sell his drawings to his family and neighbors. In 1911, his family moved once again to Kansas City. There, Walt attended the Benton Grammar School. He met Walter Pfeiffer in Kansas, who introduced him to stage plays and motion pictures. Walt started taking classes to learn art at the Kansas City Art Institute.

In 1917, Disney moved to Chicago and attended McKinley High School. He worked as a cartoonist for his school newspaper. Along with this, he started to study photography and drawing. He took night courses at the Chicago Art Institute. At the age of sixteen, Disney dropped out of school. He enrolled to join the army during World War I, but was rejected as he was underage. However, he forged a fake birth certificate and joined the Red Cross. He worked as the driver of an ambulance for the Red Cross and completed his service in 1919.

Disney began his professional career in 1919 when he moved back to Kansas City. He wanted to become a newspaper cartoonist. That year he got a job at the Pesmen-Rubin Art Studio where he created advertisements for newspapers, magazines and movie theaters.

In 1920, he found another job with the Kansas City Film Ad Company. He took an interest in animation and decided to become a cartoon artist. After he'd learned animation, he left the job to start his own company. He collaborated with Fred Harman, with whom he'd worked at the Kansas City Film Ad Company. Their first project, *Laugh-O-Grams* was very successful. The cartoon became so popular that Disney launched the Laugh-O-Gram Studio. Next, they created the short subject called *Alice in Cartoonland*. It was a seven-minute-long film. But the company struggled financially and finally shut down in 1923.

The same year, Walt and his brother started the Disney Brothers Studio in Hollywood. They began to make short animated cartoons, and even signed a deal to make more *Alice* cartoons. In 1927, the studio released the series, *Trolley Troubles* featuring the character Oswald the Lucky Rabbit.

However, in 1928, Disney came to know that Universal Pictures had trademarked Oswald. But instead of losing heart, Disney began working on creating new cartoon characters. His timeless cartoon character, Mickey Mouse, was introduced to the world in 1928, in a movie called *Steamboat Willie*. The first two animated movies were not that popular because they were silent films. However, in the third movie, he gave his own voice to the character. It was an instant hit. The cartoon became a star. The Mickey Mouse Club as well as merchandise and comics were soon created for children.

In 1929, Disney released another series called *Silly Symphonies*. The characters in the movie were Mickey's friends, Donald Duck, Goofy, Pluto and Mickey's girlfriend Minnie Mouse. The first *Silly Symphonies* cartoon made in color was called *Flowers and Trees*, in 1932. It won an Oscar. In 1933, he made another hit cartoon, *The Three Little Pigs*. Its song "Who's Afraid of the Big Bad Wolf" became an anthem for the Great Depression. It was the second animated short film to have received an

Academy Award for 'Best Animated Short Film' in 1934.

The same year, Disney began working on his feature film *Snow White and the Seven Dwarfs*. The movie was released in 1937 and won a total of eight Academy Awards. With his unceasing success, Disney brought about an era which is known as the 'Golden Age of Animation'.

In 1940, Disney released many full-length animated movies like *Pinocchio, Fantasia, Dumbo* and *Bambi*. By the 1950s Disney once again started to direct cartoon films. His first release was *Cinderella* in 1950, followed by masterpieces like *Alice in Wonderland, Peter Pan, Treasure Island, Lady and the Tramp, Sleeping Beauty* and *101 Dalmatians*.

In 1925, Walt Disney married Lillian Bound. The couple had two children. Walt Disney died on December 15, 1966, at the age of 65, due to lung cancer in Los Angeles, California.

WARREN BUFFETT

BIRTH: August 30, 1930
Omaha, Nebraska, USA

Warren Buffett is an American businessman and one of the richest men in the world. He is the CEO and the most significant shareholder of Berkshire Hathaway, and is known as the most successful investor of the twentieth century.

Warren Edward Buffett was born on August 30, 1930, in Omaha, Nebraska to Howard and Leila Stahl Buffett. His father worked as an American congressman. Warren started learning about business at a very young age and mastered the art of both money and trade. While other kids his age were busy playing, he was focused on earning money. He would sell different items door-to-door and also worked at a grocery store owned by his grandfather. Buffett started his elementary education at the Rose Hill Elementary School. He graduated from Woodrow Wilson High School in 1947.

Even as a high school student, Buffett managed to earn a good amount of money. He took many odd jobs like selling stamps, golf balls and delivering newspapers. He saved money and invested it in stocks. Buffett's interest in stock exchange grew; he'd bought his first shares by the age of eleven. One valuable thing he learned from his first investment was patience. He'd bought three shares for himself and his sister. However, soon after he bought the stock its price fell. Buffett sold the shares but soon come to regret his decision. The same shares' price shot up.

Buffett attended the University of Nebraska to pursue his higher studies. He graduated with a

Bachelor of Science degree, followed by a Master of Science from the University of Columbia in 1951. He also attended the New York Institute of Finance to learn Business.

By the age of twenty, Buffett had saved over thousands of dollars. Buffett's first proper job was at his father's company, Buffett-Falk & Co., as an investment salesman. When Buffett was a student at Columbia University, he met Benjamin Graham, from whom he learned about investments. He was ready to work for Graham for free, but was not offered a job after his training was complete. However, in 1954, Benjamin Graham called him up again and offered him a job. Buffett worked with him as a partner, but in 1956 Graham retired and ended the partnership.

By the time Buffett was 26, he had saved a considerable amount of money. In 1957, he opened Buffett Partnership Ltd., an investment partnership in Omaha. Buffett's family members and friends invested in his business. During 1960, he was engaged in seven partnerships. In 1962, Buffett became a millionaire for the first time.

Buffett made an investment in a fabric company, Berkshire Hathaway, and took control of the company. In 1973, he bought stocks in the Washington Post Company and soon became a member of the board. Buffett's reputation as a businessman was so well-established that once news spread about him buying a certain stock, its price would shoot up. Buffett bought a majority of Coca-Cola Company's shares in 1988. It proved to be one of his best investments.

Owing to his constant hard work, he had become the richest person in the world by 2008. Before him, Bill Gates had been at the top for thirteen years. Another significant investment that contributed to his success was in IBM in 2011. Buffett had purchased IBM shares worth a million dollars.

Buffett was presented with the Presidential

Medal of Freedom by President Barack Obama in 2010 for his brilliance in the investment business, but also for his charity work. In 1981, Buffett donated a huge share of his company to charity. In 2006, he donated half of his earnings from Berkshire Hathaway to five charity foundations, including the Bill and Melinda Gates Foundation. This was the biggest donation they had ever received.

Warren Buffett is the perfect role model for young entrepreneurs. He sends a clear message of vision, mission, focus and hard work. In 2018, he planned to establish a new health care company. Buffett's aim in business is to find ways to cut costs with a primary focus on technology. Buffett has managed to turn poor investments into pure gold. For this, he is known as the Oracle of Omaha.

QUESTIONS

Q.1.   Where did Mukesh Ambani study?

Q.2.   What was Berkshire Hathaway when Warren Buffett discovered the company in the early 1960s?

Q.3.   How old was Warren Buffett when he bought his first stock? Explain the investment he made.

Q.4.   Which company did Walt and his brother start in 1923?

Q.5.   What was the name of Richard Branson's first student magazine?

Q.6.   Name the Disney movies released in 1940.

Q.7.   What was Steve Jobs' first summer job and with whom?

Q.8.   After leaving Apple in 1985, which business did Steve Jobs start?

Q.9.   What is the name of Oprah's company which produces her shows?

Q.10. What was the name of the world's cheapest car that was launched by Ratan Tata?

Q.11. What is the name of Bill Gates' foundation?

Q.12. What was the name of Larry Page's other company?

Q.13. What is the name of Peter Jones' foundation? Explain its functions.

Q.14. Which corporate companies did Ratan Tata establish? Name them.

Q.15. Who is the founder of Nike Inc.?

Q.16. Who is the CEO of Starbucks? Explain its work culture.

Q.17. Which network did Oprah create to support children?

Q.18. What is Jeff Bezos' full name?

Q.19. Who co-founded Google with Larry Page?

Q.20. What is the tag line for Amazon's e-commerce store?

Q.21. What is the purpose of the Fundación Amancio Ortega foundation?

Q.22. What was the name of Mary Kay Ash's company? Mention some of its products.

Q.23. Who are Bill Gates' parents?

Q.24. When did Ray Kroc start his company which later became the biggest food chain in the world?

Q.25. Name the different coffee beverages that Howard Schultz introduced on the Starbucks menu.

Q.26. What is the slogan that Phil Knight used for Nike's promotion?

Q.27. What is the name of Amancio Ortega's company and when was it founded?

Q.28. What was the Golden Rule that Mary Kay Ash followed for her company?

Q.29. What is the name of Arianna Huffington's online news magazine?

Q.30. What was the name of Larry Page's children's books start up?

DID YOU KNOW?

1. Arianna Huffington wrote her first book about the women's liberation movement, *The Female Woman*, at the age of 22.

2. Bill Gates read the entire *World Book Encyclopedia* series in his teenage years.

3. Warren Buffett decided to donate half of his Berkshire Hathaway stocks to charitable foundations.

4. Elon Musk's 'The Falcon' rocket gets its name from *Star Wars*' Millennium Falcon.

5. From 1928 to 1947, Walt Disney voiced Mickey Mouse himself.

6. Mukesh Ambani is the owner of the world's largest refinery situated in Jamnagar in Gujarat.

7. Walt Disney created many children's television programs such as *Zorro* and *The Mickey Mouse Club*.

8. Arianna Huffington was already five-foot-ten when she was thirteen. "I was excluded from the school parade because I was too tall," Arianna recalls.

9. Warren Buffett earned 94% of his wealth after he turned sixty.

10. Mark Zuckerberg founded CourseMatch for Harvard students, to help them pick classes based on the classes their friends were enrolled in.

11. As a child, Oprah Winfrey was nicknamed "The Preacher". She would recite Bible verses all the time.

12. Henry Ford was inspired by Edison to build cars. In 1896, Ford met Thomas Edison, who approved of the Ford automobile blueprints.

13. Google was originally named BackRub by Larry Page.

14. Oprah Winfrey launched Oxygen Media to produce cable programs specifically for women.

15. Google's first office was a rented garage.